MW01247238

From the Balcony

New Perspectives for The Old Power Games!

From the Balcony, New Perspectives for Old Power Games, Toni Lynn Chinoy

2nd edition

Dedication:

To Ann McLaughlin who asked for her very own version, Marc who believed that this work was important, and last but not least, to my clients who work so hard to live their principles in very tough environments. Without them and their courage, the content of this book could not exist.

Foreword

Power Games are inevitable. You cannot escape them.

Do you dread the days you know that you will interact with specific individuals? Do you find yourself weeping at the thought of going to work? Do you wish you had a suit of armor to protect you from the viscous dialogue you may have to engage in, in order to express an idea? Are you driven into rage by the unfair misrepresentations of your behaviors by others?

Unfortunately, too many of us are driven to thug-like behavior by the Games others play. We become angry, restless, argumentative and frustrated, even while we believe ourselves to be civilized and controlled. The most unfortunate aspect of Power Games is the amount of energy consumed for something frivolous and unproductive which could and should be channeled into productivity.

If you observe animals as they interact, it is often easy to identify their dance to determine which will dominate and under what circumstance. We call it Pecking Order.

In humans, *Power Games* are the dance of Pecking Order.

This book is dedicated to giving you the "Balcony" view of your interactions so that you may choose your responses to the Power Games more wisely. With a different perspective based on mathematical models, your own Power Games can appear as ridiculous and destructive to you as they do to others who are observing. They often appear far more silly, far more of a waste of time and energy, and far more disruptive than they do when you are in the midst of trying to preserve your turf, your plan, your dignity, or your ego!

In order to create a different world for yourself where effort is focused on results rather than Pecking Order, you owe it to yourself to evolve your understanding of both Power and of the Games. You may want to learn how to leverage your effort to create an outcome of Quality instead of battling for position.

Along with a new perspective, *From the Balcony* will offer alternatives for responding to the unwelcome attacks of others. The techniques represented in this text follow from an understanding of nature that is illustrated in a simple statement by a very wise riding instructor, Albrecht von Ziegner, "When attempting to master a twelve hundred pound horse, make the right things easy, and the wrong things difficult."

Why not? Why would you attempt to 'strong arm' a twelve hundred pound animal when you can outsmart him? The mission of *From the Balcony* is to help you outsmart the bullies by making it easy for them to do the "right" things!

T.L.C.

Contents

Overview

Book I

The Forces

Book II

What to Do About Bullies!

Appendix

BOOK I

The Forces

One

Power Games

What is a Power Game?

A Power Game may be either the most refined or the most blatant of attempts to establish dominance between any two individuals or groups of individuals. It can be as simple as controlling the conversation or as complicated as manipulating a series of deals.

Wrong and right is generally not the issue for most Power Games.

'Who's in control?' is the issue.

Power Games are most often played according to Street Rules. It is sometimes difficult to tell the Leaders from the Bullies when they are engaged in a Power Game. They all look the same, and everybody looks BAD.

Participation in the Games is often both mindless and destructive. We are compelled. Together, we create the endless divorce, the Enron collapse, or the continuous cultural wars of our planet.

What Rules?

A game is an activity involving *competition* under *rules.* The point of many games is to anticipate the other player, and to respond appropriately. Additionally, the point is to be in control of the play by directing the action in the way that benefits you, and your team, most.

One of the biggest issues of Power Games is that the rules are unclear and vary from person to person. If you want to play the Games more effectively, you will want to become more astute at understanding the rules under which the other person is playing as well as their objectives for any engagement.

You will also want to spend some time and effort understanding what rules you should hold yourself accountable to in order to improve your success.

There are many individuals who operate at a distinct disadvantage in the most of ruthless of Power Games because they have been ill-prepared to cope with the realities of their environment. There are some obvious clues that you may be operating at a disadvantage. Check any or all of the answers below if you recognize yourself.

Symptoms of not being well prepared to play the Game. Check those that apply to you!

- ❑ I get surprised by the lack of professionalism I see in my peers.
- ❑ I am amazed at self-serving agendas, particularly when the organization is in crisis.
- ❑ I expect others to do the right thing in tough situations.
- ❑ I have been surprised at becoming a target for no apparent reason.
- ❑ I cannot believe that some of the mediocre people I work with have made it this far.
- ❑ I am weary from having to fight so hard just to do what seems so obvious to me.
- ❑ I am surprised at the lack of respectful behavior among my peers.
- ❑ I cannot understand why a person who is mediocre seems to get the support of the hierarchy in the organization.

The first thing you must understand in order to become more effective is that, in the midst of a Game, there are many who will bend reality to meet their personal needs. If you are in the middle of a nasty Power Game, and if you are hoping for the Games to go away, or your opponents to be fired or some equally serendipitous resolution, get over it. You cannot opt out of the Games, so you may as well learn how to play.

Don't be surprised to find that the higher you climb in the food chain, the nastier it gets. The stakes are higher. It may actually become *more* common for others to manipulate, lie, bully.

"Grow Up" if You Expect to Succeed

Righteous is useless. Too many strong leaders fall into this trap. Being surprised, amazed, angry are symptoms that you are naive. There is no place for naive Leadership. Your escape into righteous or indignant behavior is simply a diversion from the need to grow and understand what is happening around you.

You may feel that you have no choice. If so, you have become a victim. Perhaps, as a result you are choosing to compromise what you believe to be right in the interest of surviving.

You always have choice. It is simply a matter of how you perceive your risks and how you respond to them. And, that is the purpose of this book. To identify what is really happening (as opposed to what you believe *should* be happening), and then to offer alternatives to caving-in or playing dead.

Prepare for the Games by Understanding What is Really Happening?

Power Games are an exchange of energy. Each time a Game is played out, it has an overall effect on the entire ecosystem of relationships. The magnitude of the effect is determined by the Force and Direction brought to the Game by the players.

When you give Power to those who have gaps in honor, integrity, generosity, and fairness, you are giving control to the bullies, the whiners, the manipulators, the phonies and the liars. Their forces are greater than yours and they are directing the outcomes of the Games toward the culture in which they are most comfortable.

It is tough to play against those who have no boundaries and perhaps no morals. You *can* play to win, and do so without compromising who you are.

Two

Redefining the Games

Taking Charge

According to Webster's Dictionary, "Energy is an inherent Power capacity for action." When an interaction is completed between two individuals, their combined energy must take on a new magnitude as well as a new direction. The newly directed energy is a result of the separate forces brought into the interaction by each person.

In other words, there is a new "inherent Power capacity for action." This new "inherent Power capacity for action" is loaded with potential for influencing the outcome of the Game.

In order to take control of the direction of any given Power exchange, you should first identify the principles behind the interactions and the forces which determine the nature, degree, and quality of the outcomes. You can then choose to apply a different set of behaviors to a Power Game. The purpose is to create the most *positive* capacity for action, rather than the least.

Two Kinds of Power

There are *two* forms of Power brought into the Games by its participants. They are *Personal Power* and *Positional Power*.

The biggest misconception from which many players in the Power Games suffer is the illusion that Strength (Positional Power) is the key factor in determining the outcome. Just because she or he's your boss, or has a higher rank in the organization does not mean she or he will ultimately win any Power Game.

Positional Power represents your acquired status (rank) in the situation. It might include how much influence you have, how much influence your friends have, to what degree you are expert in your situation, etc. It can also depend on how the other person perceives your status.

Personal Power, the other form of Power, is the amount of wisdom and balance you bring to the Game. It is made up of many factors including how well you listen, how respectful you are of the other person, how patient you are in letting things unfold, how balanced you are, your self-esteem, and others. We will describe both Positional Power and Personal Power in depth in later chapters.

The reason the Games are what they are and take the toll that they do, is because of our reverence for *Positional Power* and our lack of understanding of *Personal Power*!

Why is Personal Power so Important?

Wisdom is often neglected by very smart people who get caught in the arm-wrestling contests which seem to proliferate around Power Games. They are reacting instinctively rather than tapping into their own Personal Power.

Think of the outcome of any Power Game in this way. The more *Personal Power* (Wisdom) brought to the Game by individual players, the better the QUALITY of the outcome. The more *Positional Power* brought to the Game by the individual players, the more force available to EXECUTE an outcome.

Frequently, Personal Power and Positional Power are handled as opposing forces instead of as an integration of two dimensions of decision-making. Individuals will often abdicate Personal Power with its inherent qualities of courage, honesty and integrity, in favor of

Positional Power which might include wealth, position, status, or job security.

Some Issues Around Personal Power

Because Personal Power is so important to the Quality of the outcome, it is crucial that you do not misunderstand its nature and how it works. There are many *inappropriate* definitions for Personal Power.

For example, a person may incorrectly define Personal Power as his or her mental prowess. That person may have received positive feedback for years about how smart he or she is, only to find out in his or her advanced career that some of the same people offering praise perceived the self-same intelligence as a form of arrogance.

A person's belief in his or her own excellence accompanied by an arrogant attitude may actually diminish the individual's Personal Power. This is potentially devastating in his or her ability to influence others. And, after all, positively influencing others is what Leadership is all about. Some of the most disappointing career setbacks stem from arrogance.

Perhaps you know talented people, who in their own righteousness, have ruined or stagnated their careers. Perhaps you are one.

Talented individuals are often naive about what it means to be successful as they near the top. They assume that they will continue to be rewarded for their contribution and that the rules of advancement are the same as they were earlier in their careers.

Leadership is never done in a vacuum. Being smart is not enough. Many people with wonderful skills, knowledge and insight reach an early plateau with their careers and are mystified. It is most often a misunderstanding of Personal Power that causes the stagnation.

14

Charisma/Personal Power?

Another misconception around Personal Power occurs with the assumption that Personal Power is a kind of charisma. Charisma and personal charm are only a small part of Personal Power, offset by other equally important elements.

If one possesses charisma without the attending wisdom, integrity, and courage, the outcome of the Power Games are often destructive in nature. The need to be liked and adored may come at a huge price.

A Few Misconceptions About Positional Power

There are some equally misleading conceptions about the nature of Positional Power. If you assume that higher rank which is often equated with more control will automatically provide you a greater ability to affect key outcomes, you may be disappointed.

The world is loaded with high level executives who continue to struggle as much as they did at the lower levels to be heard and to be respected. When this is the case, there may be something else wrong!

Three

Positional Power

Components of Positional Power

The *essence* of Positional Power is the amount of **Situational Force** an individual can bring to bear on the outcome of an exchange.

There are three main components to Positional Power. If you understand them and learn how to work with them, you can leverage the amount of positional (situational) force you bring to an interaction. At times, the ability to leverage Positional Power offers an advantage, particularly if it is combined with Personal Power.

What are the elements which give Positional Power its value? As you read the following elements, think about a person who is using his or her Position to intimidate or thwart you and ask if you are maximizing your own Positional Power in this situation.

I.   Your capacity to manage perceptions (both yours and others') of Positional Power.

- Your rank or status in the interaction
- The perception others have of that rank in this situation (It does not matter what you think of your rank if others are unimpressed.)
- The circumstance surrounding the interaction you are focusing on.
- Your own perception of your rank and its attending power. (Absolutely key to changing the outcome)
- The circumstance surrounding the interaction

II.　Your capacity to manage Knowledge

- Are you an "expert" around the topic of the interaction? (For example, if you are legal counsel for an organization and there is a lawsuit pending, they may be willing to pay more attention to you than they did when you were trying to warn them not to get into the situation in the first place.)
- Do others perceive you as an expert?

III.　Your capacity to manage networks

- What are the connections you have that may positively affect this circumstance?
- How well are you able to utilize that network in relationship to this circumstance?

Note:　A person's Positional Power in an interaction is influenced by:

1.　Its relativity to the other person's Positional Power.

2.　The wisdom (Personal Power) with which it is applied!

How to Use this Information

Identify the things that affect your Positional Power and leverage them. In any specific situation, ask yourself the telling questions. What is your expertise? Can you enhance it for this situation in order to gain Positional Power?

Who's in your network? Do you need to do a better job of setting that up? Are your relationships what they should be in this situation? Do you need to fix them?

Are you confident about your Positional Power or apologetic? Do you assume that you will get what you want or do you assume that you will have to fight for it?

What do you do when you have very little Positional Power in a situation where you should have extensive Positional Power? Have you ever been bullied by someone who is supposed to be serving you? Ever had a clerk in a store act as though you were taking up too much time, a secretary keep you off the schedule of her boss, a subordinate who questioned everything you said?

The options we have in changing the balance of Power reside in the understanding and use of the elements of Positional Power and Personal Power. If you want to change your Positional Power, the correct pressure points for doing so are in the three categories identified above.

Positional Power and Rank

It is very important that you do not assume that increasing Rank will solve your problems. Rank is only one aspect of Positional Power. Many high ranking people turn into victims when confronted with the wrong personality.

How you use your rank, what you believe about it, and what others perceive about you will determine your force in any Power Game.

Four

Personal Power

The last chapter identified the elements of *Positional Power* on which you can focus to diagnose why you are having trouble with an interaction. It also identifies those elements that you may change to affect the outcome.

If you really want to change your life, however, knowing and understanding the elements affecting your *Personal Power* is a valuable use of your time and energy. It is through managing your Personal Power that you may have the most dramatic impact on the outcome of your interaction with others.

Components of Personal Power

Personal Power is an indication of how much **wisdom** you bring to the Game. As you examine these questions, consider any interaction in your personal or professional life which is going badly.

I.	Your ability to Manage Fear

- In this interaction or circumstance, are you able to stay calm and objective?
- In this situation, are you or would you, be able to take feedback about your choices, even though the other person is clearly wrong?
- In relation to this person or this situation, how would you rate your self-esteem if you were evaluating your behavior as an outsider?

- Is your sense of Timing appropriate or are you either too slow or too fast in regard to this situation? How would you know?

II.   Your ability to Manage Confusion

- Are you able to be completely honest with yourself and others regarding this interaction or this person with whom you are involved in a Power Game?
- How would you evaluate your integrity (your ability to do the right thing no matter how angry, abused, or intimidated you are) in this situation?
- Do you have an ability to listen openly and objectively to the other party's point of view in this situation?
- Are you clear about the cause and effect relationships surrounding this circumstance? In other words, do you know what specifically you have done to create this reality? Are you willing to look at the unfolding circumstance in that way?

III.   Your Ability to Manage Arrogance

- Are you able to look at shifts in circumstance as a cycle without panicking or overreacting or do you have a need to *always* be perceived as a winner? Are you afraid to respond authentically and appropriately because of the potential for triggering a negative impact on your life?
- Do you think and act in a way that is thoughtful about the long-term implications of your choices?
- In the midst of the Power Game, do you still attempt to meet the personal needs of the other party? Do you know when to stop trying to meet them?

- Are you able to make decisions for the good of the entire ecosystem, rather than for personal agendas and ego needs. Do you know how to take care of yourself?

Imagine that you bring a Force into every interaction. You will want to increase the magnitude of that Force in order to gain more favorable results in the Game. If you want to increase the amount of force you bring into a Power Game, there are many leverage points to be found within the categories and questions listed above.

It is very difficult to remain objective when it comes to your own Personal Power. It is much easier to see the flaws in others. There are so many subtle influences of which you may be unaware. For example, your beliefs about relationships may complicate your ability to act with good judgement and wisdom in a tricky situation.

You may instinctively try to protect relationships that have no merit with individuals who have no intention of preserving or protecting the same relationship. Your ability to see and respond to the quality of the relationship *as it is,* rather than as you would like it to be, is often a test of your Personal Power.

In a later chapter we will be more specific about how to rate your performance on the above fundamentals. If however, you perceive any relationship or interaction to be broken, a focus on the fundamentals of Personal Power will always improve the situation.

Five

How Do Power Games Work?

Are you a victim to other people's attacks? Do you know how to handle a Bully with grace and firmness? Are you swallowing your responses because the other person has more Positional Power than you?

Have you ever become speechless and allowed others to abuse you because you don't know how defend yourself? Do you sometimes contort yourself so that others will like you or believe you to be fair and measured, even when you want to do something more intense and more clear?

In the midst of our conflicts, we may be quick to blame others for our struggle. We are often completely unaware of our own choices and how they impact the reality we create for ourselves. We need a distant and more objective lense for viewing our results and ourselves.

Using Vector Analysis: the objective view

In any interaction, there is an observable and discernable energy between individuals and groups. If one is sensitized to the forms and directions of that energy, a person may begin to define the Power (direction *and* level of influence) occurring in the engagement.

The category of mathematics called Vector Analysis provides an interesting framework for discussing the Power exchange in any interaction between two individuals (or any two or more groups), and a potential for evaluating the consequence of that exchange. That evaluation offers information which will help you to determine where the greatest leverage points for positive change exist.

Vector is a derivation of the word vehere (to carry). A vector in mathematics can be a means for identifying a *directional force*. If we think of the vector, or arrow, as an indicator of both the *direction* of the energy and the *force* with which it is delivered, we will then be able (through *simple* mathematical exercise) to assess the result of any Power exchange.

Forces represented by arrows indicating both the direction and the magnitude of your force can be graphed and then manipulated to identify their impact on each other and on the whole.

Ideally, in any exchange of Power, there is an *optimal* form where the most positive outcome is maximized.

Conversely, there are sub-optimal forms, in which the outcomes are less than ideal.
Our view of the Power Game becomes less subjective once we are able to segment behavior into smaller and smaller increments. For that reason, as we determine values for a person's Power vectors, we will follow an incremental process comparable to finding the length of a curve in Calculus.

To do so, you simply take those categories for Positional and Personal Power outlined in the last two chapters and ask specific questions about each of them to further differentiate and ultimately measure a person's performance in the Game.

Measuring Your Force

How do you affect the size of your arrow, as well as be clearer about the direction in which you are attempting to push?

In other words, "How do I get stronger?", and "How do I know what direction to push to have the most leverage?"

To understand the answers to that, we will take matters in two stages.

1)   What are the *directions* for Power Games and what do they mean in terms of the result?

2)   What elements affect the strength (as reflected in the size of the arrow.)

Six

Direction of a Power Game

How Do You Know If the Game is Going in a Positive or Negative Direction?

To determine if the direction is positive or negative, you need to have a good set of rules. If you didn't have a goal post assigned to your team, how would you know if you were moving the ball in a positive or negative direction?

The following rules represent a set of circumstances which will determine for our purposes whether the Game (outcome of your force against the other person's force) is moving in a positive or negative direction.

Rules for the Games

1) **To win, the overall well-being of the organization, friendship, or relationship must be enhanced by the outcome of the Game.**

2) **To win, both the productivity and the energy of the organization must be improved as a result of the Game.**

3) **To win, each individual (not just you) involved in the Game must be fulfilled as a result of playing the Game. You do not win (by our rules) if others are diminished as a result of you and *your* actions. NOTE: the other party can choose to diminish him or herself by the choices he or she makes, but your actions are never chosen to diminish the other person!**

---

4) Ego and personal agendas are viewed as negative influencers of the Power Game when they become more important than the overall well-being of the organization.

5) Wisdom and Personal Power are more important attributes to winning than are rank and position when used appropriately.

6) Courage is necessary to win Power Games. The organization is never improved by self-serving, safe responses to threats.

Premise: The overall circumstance may not have improved as much as you would like it to improve for the outcome of the Game to still qualify as a positive result (WIN). The engagement must move the organization toward a better outcome than what was occurring was when the interaction started.

Influencing the Game

A simple (x,y) graph will serve as a frame for the interaction with $(0,0)$ being the starting point for all Power Games.

Let x=Position and y=Personal Power.

Following the basic (x,y) graph where y is the vertical axis and x is horizontal, it might look like the following:

A Simple (x,y) Graph

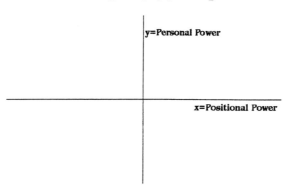

Each person's Power Vector will be represented by an arrow that starts at (0,0) (the center) and falls into one of the four quadrants represented by this (x,y) graph.

The first quadrant (top right) is where *both* x and y are positive. A person who has both *positive x* (Positional Power) and *positive y* (Personal Power) will have a vector which falls in the first quadrant. This is where the *Leaders* are found.

In the quadrant on the bottom right, x is always *positive* (Positional Power) and y (Personal Power) is always *negative*. Any individual whose personal Vector determined by his or her x and y values falls into that quadrant should be considered a *Bully*.

If a person's vector falls into the bottom left quadrant, that means his or her x (Positional Power) is *negative* and his or her y (Personal

Power) is also *negative*. Bad news. Such a placement indicates that the person is acting as a *Victim*.

The last quadrant, the top left quadrant, is where a person's x value is *negative* (low Positional Power) and his or her y value is *positive*. Through his or her wisdom, in spite of a lack of Positional Power, this person is showing a high potential is designated as a "Star". If nurtured, this individual will have a very positive impact on an organization.

Four Quadrants for Depicting Power Vectors

The upper right quadrant is the most important quadrant for defining successful outcomes for the organization. It is there that you are mostly likely to find evidence of the achievement of meaningful goals (i.e.: the rules for Power Games are all met). This is the only quadrant in which both x and y are positive. Any of the other quadrants highlight deficiencies in how a person has interacted in terms of his or her Power.

How Interactions Affect the Outcome

To use the vectors, it is important to see what happens when *two* individuals interact. It is through interaction that we see the combined result and its affect on the organization.

Suppose you are interacting with a Bully. You know this person is a Bully without a graph. What you may not realize is how your interactions with this person affect the organization and how much responsibility *you* have for the quality of the result.

If a Leader and a Bully are interacting, they are exerting a force on each other. How do you know where it will end up? The resulting vector will depend on who is exerting more force and in which direction. In every case, they *will* affect each other.

The way you can demonstrate what has occurred is by adding the opposing forces and displaying the results on a graph. The resulting force of two vectors is the diagonal of the completed Parallelogram formed by finishing the parallelogram started by your two existing vectors. (You can add the endpoints of the two existing vectors to find the diagonal as well). The following graph offers an example of the interaction between a Bully and a Leader. The endpoints are for the time being, arbitrary.

Bully and Leader Interact

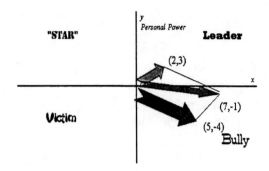

In this case, because the Bully had a larger absolute numerical value of his x and y (even though his y is negative), he has dragged the outcome (the resulting force) of the interaction into the Bully quadrant. His force is greater than the Leader's force. In terms of results to the organization, this interaction has caused the culture of the organization to fall into the Bully quadrant. You may believe yourself to be above reproach, but you are a participant in a Game that is adversely affecting the whole.

What Does it Mean for you?

If you would like to be more effective in specific Power Games, the graphs hold some interesting answers.

It may benefit you to understand what is actually happening in a Power Game and which components of the Game drive its results.

Seven

Defining Winners and Losers

You may already understand how to spot the winners and losers of a Power Game. The loser is the one with the long face and the winner is smug. Unfortunately, it is not that simple. The time frame has a lot to do with determining winners and losers.

The rules, as defined in Chapter Six, are very important in determining winners and losers of Power Games. For example, there are many bullies who exude enough magnitude in their force to drag the results of the Game to their agenda. If that agenda is ultimately bad for the organization or bad for individuals, the bully will **never** be a winner, no matter how he or she looks temporarily. If you are patient enough to watch over a long period of time, Bullies always "get theirs".

The winner of a Power Game is not necessarily the one who gets his or her way. A true "winner" of Power Games is the person who moves with grace and a definite sense of direction toward a positive outcome for the whole.

The winner *(as we are defining it here)* never loses sight of the objective of a more productive whole. As a result, the winner of a Power Game is always in the process of creating more harmony, higher energy, and less chaos.

Winning is getting to live in an environment that reflects those outcomes.

Too many "wanna be" leaders get sucked into fighting for their own agenda in ways that cause them to lose the ultimate rewards of "winning" which are related to the most positive outcome for the organization.

The ultimate test of winning and losing is a realistic assessment of your reality. Are you living a peaceful and graceful existence or are you living with the outcome of your own bad choices in your engagements in Power Games? The more peaceful and productive your reality, the better a player you are. Of course, the opposite is also true. If you find that your existence is one painful battle after another, you are a "loser".

Losers of Power Games may become Victims at the moment they should stand up for what is right, become *Bullies* when they should be listening and cooperating, or they may abdicate action by assuming that their day will come when they have the Positional Power to match their clever and brilliant assessment of what should be done. There are lots of ways to lose and only a few ways to win.

Example: The Lose/ Lose Scenario

Often a source of enlightenment for talented leaders, the graphs will show the outcome of some very common battles.

Imagine for a moment that you are feeling betrayed by someone who you believe should have the same goals and objectives you do. You are dumbfounded. How could this person do this? Why would this person do this? This is a Power Game.

If you want to explore and evolve your leadership ability, there is a hard lesson you must absorb.

Real Leadership is *never* naive.

Leadership is *always* lonely.

Stop being surprised. The higher you go, the bigger the stakes, the more likely you will become a target by people you know, and often people you trust.

Imagine that you are involved in a Game with a Bully. You think of yourself as a leader, but you react to the attacks of the other person with increasing rage. Your increasing frustration is disabling you and unfortunately, you fall into the category of Victim. You cannot seem to react appropriately and your anger clouds your ability to think clearly about what is happening. The situation feels more and more out of control. You even feel like a Victim.

Bully and a Victim Interact

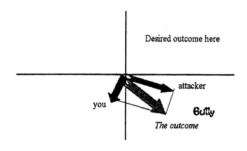

The diagonal is the sum of your interaction. What is this interaction doing to the organization? Together, you are establishing a relationship based on bullying and the outcome is an even more negative result than either of you bring into the interaction. The QUALITY of the interaction, regardless of who wins or loses, is very low in terms of the culture of the whole.

As a result, although this battle was about dominance, even if the Bully wins, what has he won? Also, if the rest of the organization's model of relationships is one of observing one executive bullying another, guess what the organization learns? It does not take anyone long to figure out that optimists and idea people are for bullying, and this organization now has a second universe of issues.

The Point?

Power Games do not happen in a vacuum. Their impact, good or bad, has an impact on the whole. If you are a participant in any Power Game in which the resulting vector falls in a *victim* or *bully* quadrant, you have impacted the culture of the whole in a negative way.

It takes two vectors to get a result in *any* quadrant.

Change the graph, you change the organization. Continue the game for dominance, and you continue to destroy the unit. Whether you are the Bully or the Victim, you have a responsibility to step back, hold yourself accountable, and change the result!

A Bully and a Victim interacting cast a pall on the entire organization. Productivity and efficiency are greatly diminished in such a culture.

If you are the bully, even if you believe that your way is the right way and no one knows as much as you about how things should be done, you are still being destructive. Rationalize if you will, but you are creating a culture in which it is not safe to be around you. If you are the boss *and* a bully, you have damaged your organization, and you will pay for it in performance.

Suppose either of these two characters change in some way related to his or her Personal Power (listening better, less fearful, more balanced in his or her response).

In any exchange, if both were to change simple things related to Personal Power, the resulting change would change the outcome for the organization or unit in a significant way. Our Bully, Victim vectors might look more like the graph below.

What a Difference!

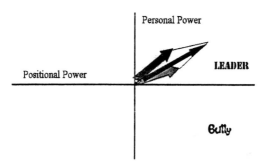

Again, the diagonal is the result of their interaction. By the Bully's appreciating the optimist's contribution and being open and respectful, the dynamic changes for the organization. Each person takes responsibility for his or her behavior.

How likely is it that the Bully will change his or her behavior or that the Victim will suddenly develop self-esteem?

If *only* one person changes, the outcome still changes to one that is healthier for the organization. The individual who chooses to do the work to change only themselves in a Power Game, ultimately reaps rewards for doing so. The career and life changes that occur because a victim learns how not to be a victim are well worth striving for.

The bully may continue to be a Bully, but the victim is no longer available.

The next chapter will dive into the specifics of how to assign x and y values for your own Personal Power Vector. In doing so, we will begin to identify how to change the results of the Games and the force that you wield in your own interactions.

Eight

Manipulating the Games

For those of you who hate the graphs and the charts, you will still *want* to understand this chapter. This chapter identifies, clearly and distinctly, why additional Positional Power is NOT the answer to your problems.

The following is a graph that we showed in Chapter VI . The x axis (horizontal) is Positional Power, and the y axis (vertical) is Personal Power.

Bully and Leader Interact

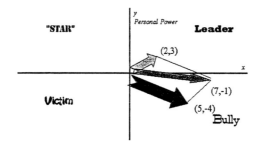

The diagonal was the result of the Bully interacting with the Leader. The Bully pulled the interaction for the organization into the Bully quadrant. This means that in spite of the Leader's input, the organization observes a Bully dominating the situation and the response is to become fearful and tentative to the Bully.

What if the Leader in this situation got a promotion and now outranks the Bully? What if he did not change his Personal Power (did not improve the quality of his interaction with the Bully), but his Positional Power (x) has now increased due to the promotion?

This would have the effect of keeping y the same while x becomes greater. The new Power Vector for our Leader would be longer in the x direction but would not go any further up the y scale on the graph. Our Bully's vector stays exactly the same. The resulting graph with these changes is below.

Bully and Leader Interact

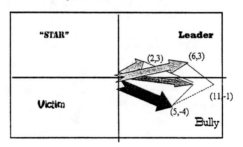

This is key to your understanding of the Games. The new endpoint of the new diagonal formed by giving our Leader a larger x value is (11,-1).

Notice, the result is still in the same quadrant as it was before. The new diagonal of a parallelogram showing the interaction now that we have a new x value of 6 has exactly the same y value of -1 as it did before. The outcome has a bigger x than before (more oomph) but the Quality of the outcome is still a negative y (same low wisdom applied to the decision).

Changing your Positional Power is only really helpful if it is accompanied by an increase in Personal Power. (See below)

How Do You Work With These Fundamentals?

If you want to make your Personal Power Component larger (which would drive the direction of the arrow upward), you should do so by paying attention to the fundamentals which affect Personal Power (listening skills, setting boundaries, respectful behavior, etc.).

If you would score yourself low on any of those fundamentals, that fundamental automatically becomes a place for you to focus. On the assumption that your overall ambition is to move the entire interaction into a more healthy position for the organization and ultimately for you, you may have to trust that to do so will move the overall, or long-term outcome for *you* into a better position as well.

Assume for a moment that you are the Leader in your Power Game. Totally objective review places your Vector in the Leadership quadrant.

(NOTE: there are specific questions regarding the fundamentals of Positional and Personal Power, with values attached to determine the numerical values of x and y for any interactions. If you would like to look ahead, you will find a copy of the questions in the Appendix at the end of the book.)

You may be thinking, "I am a Leader. Why should *I* change? Why should I try to raise my Personal Power values? After all, he is the one who is the Bully."

Here's why. You have no control over him. You have control over you. And you want a better outcome for the organization.

This is the hardest part of changing your reality. To change the outcome for the whole, you may have to change, even when you think you are right. If you practice listening better (yes, we know he is a jerk), stay calmer, remain objective, let go of fear, and in general, simply focus on what you *can* change, you are likely to see a very different outcome for the organization (and ultimately for you).

If *you*, the Leader, raise your score for Personal Power, leave your Positional Power the same, and he does not change at all, what happens to the outcome? By changing y from 3 to a 5, the new endpoint of the new diagonal becomes (7,1).

Why should *you* change?

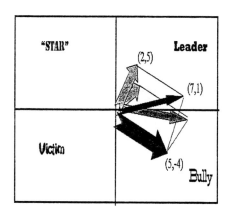

It did ***not*** help the outcome when we gave the Leader more *Positional Power* (see last graph-resulting vector stayed in same quadrant). It *did* help the outcome for the organization when you raised your *Personal Power*. For the moment, you may see no pay off for you (personally) in such an effort. Read on.

You may feel overwhelmed or angry and therefore justify behaviors that create an outcome for the organization that is more negative than either your behavior, or your *opponent's* behavior. If you were to let go of being right, let go of winning and focus simply on creating the best outcome for the organization, results change for you personally as well as for the organization.

Why? Because when the organization wins, everyone anywhere near it wins. So often we get lost in rationalizing or justifying our choices.

It is pointless. The outcome is still the outcome. Anyone anywhere near a bad outcome, loses.

You should make a decision that you are going to let go of being the Victim in these scenarios, or your overall reality probably will not change.

How?

You change the outcome by adjusting those areas where you are weak. This is particularly effective for the organization if you are able to adjust the elements of Personal Power. How do you do that?

First, you score yourself in the fundamentals (outlined in Chapter Three and Four) in order to determine where you are weak. How do you score yourself? You answer a set of questions around the 8 fundamentals for Positional Power and around the 12 fundamentals for Personal Power.

You will find the complete set of questions in the Appendix. An example of the questions you will answer is:

To what extent is this person able to remain unafraid and relaxed in this situation?

relaxed and fearless	10
somewhat relaxed and unafraid	5
not at all	- 5
tense and fearful	-10

Let's say you are answering this question about yourself. If you give yourself a score of less than 10, you know that this is a place you should focus to raise your Personal Power value. Each question offers that potential. When you add them up and take an average, you have an approximation of the value of your Personal Power Coordinate. When you do the same for the questions associated with Positional Power, you will find a relative value for how you handle your Positional Power.

You are probably going to be biased and think your opponent does everything badly and you do mostly well. The value of understanding Vector Analysis and the fundamentals of Positional and Personal Power, is to raise your awareness of your *own* weaknesses and the impact on the organization of *you* making changes in you.

This is not easy. The next section of the book offers specific examples of how to handle situations to improve the scores and the Power Vectors of the whole, while improving your personal situation. Techniques are more helpful once you know what you are working on.

BOOK II

WHAT TO DO WITH BULLIES?

What to Do With Bullies

This section of the book focuses on a range of real life issues that affect the most common Power Games. It is one thing to understand what is happening and why. It is another to know the right thing to do to create the outcome you want.

It is often very helpful in terms of redirecting a Power Game to understand which Power Game you have entered. This section will offer you a menu of some of the most crude Games, as well as a method for using the Vector approach to resolve it in your favor. You will find techniques as well as logical reasons for using the techniques described.

This entire section could appropriately be titled "Managing Bullies Effectively" since the reason you feel pain in most Power Games is because you seem to be powerless to the other person's behavior.

Losing might result in the following realities for you:

Losing Looks Like:

❏ Being treated disrespectfully.
❏ Feeling angry and humiliated by the other person's abuse.
❏ Knowing that the other person's plan of action is damaging, destructive, or simply ineffective and not being able to do anything about it.
❏ Being taken advantage of repeatedly and with little or no appreciation for your contribution.
❏ Feeling forced or coerced to do things that are against your values or principles.

❏ Feeling a constant sense of insecurity as though the other person might pull the rug out from under you at any moment.
❏ Having that sense that you are rolling along and suddenly, the other person's sneakiness has taken control out of your hands.

Physical Symptoms of Losing a Power Game may include:

- grinding of teeth
- clenching of jaw
- anger
- tears
- stomach twisting
- ulcers
- head aches
- increased blood pressure

You are tired of the feeling that interacting with specific individuals or in general, is a battle.

That's why the elements of both Positional Power and Personal Power are important. When you understand them well enough to maneuver or leverage their impact, you begin to have the means to control the outcome of the Games.

There are payoffs to learning to play the Games differently. As you learn that the most effective answer to Bullies is not to respond in kind, but to assess and improve your own response, you may find that your reality changes in the following ways:

Payoffs:

❑ You no longer take the destructive behavior of others personally. You are able to stay peaceful even as you respond in a more constructive manner.

❑ You become less of a target for Bullies and their manipulations.

❑ You experience more healthy interactions with others.

❑ You set clearer boundaries and, as a result, experience more control over your life, your time, and your experiences.

❑ You gain a clearer sense of who you are and what is important to you. You become more effective at the communication of your values.

❑ You will have less need to please others by turning yourself into a pretzel.

This section focuses on common Power Games and responses which would raise your x and y values in some of the Games which may be causing you the most stress.

If you would like to personally focus on specific ways to improve your Personal and Positional Power, take any given circumstance and answer the questions on Positional and Personal Power located in the Appendix of this text. Find your weak areas and go to work. There is also a Work Book designed to help you look at your own unique circumstance.

Nine

Boundary Issues

Why Boundary Issues?

Many Power Games with serious consequences begin with an individual's inability to set appropriate boundaries. If you are unaware or unconscious of the need to set more acceptable limits on others regarding your space and needs, you may be attracting unwanted Power Games.

Definition of Boundary Issues

Boundary issues are Power Games about Dominance. They are a form of abuse in which one person tries to control another person's space and experience. Boundary issues form an umbrella over many abusive Power Games. Therefore, the explanations for this chapter will be slightly more detailed than the following chapters.

Boundary Issues often appear to be something else. For example, inappropriate bursts of anger may be the beginning of a more serious Power Game. The person seems to be overreacting, but what he or she may be doing is testing your boundaries to see what you will tolerate. Over time, this person may act disrespectful in other ways because you did not have a reaction to the anger.

Many people use helpfulness as a way of penetrating someone's boundaries. "Let me carry your groceries" is a way that many rapists have crossed the first boundary with their victim. A parent may loan the child money or assistance and then use his or her helpfulness as a rationale for interfering in the child's life.

48

As people interact, they often step on an imaginary line that the other person has drawn around his or her comfort zone. Because everyone's comfort zone is different, it is often difficult to tell where the line is. Each of us is bound to make some sort of mistake from time to time with Boundaries.

There is, however, a kind of individual who intentionally tramples all over the lines of others. He or she is working his or her own agenda and is deliberately, or arrogantly, being disrespectful ("my issue is more important than your boundaries"). One reason it is so confusing is because the victim of the abuse often does not realize that the Game is about Boundaries.

Symptoms

How do you know if you are in the middle of a destructive Power Game about boundaries? By the way you feel! There is a feeling of being violated that attends serious boundary games. Trust yourself. If you are feeling a sense of intrusion or violation, you are probably in the Game. By the time you feel annoyed or concerned, the game may have been going on for some time. That's one of the problems with boundary games. You don't really see the person's conduct as a violation of your boundaries until the situation has escalated to a point where it gets your attention.

Boundary issues often occur around normal interactions and it is sometimes difficult to know if your reaction is to a boundary issue. You may struggle to justify why what seems appropriate behavior from one person feels inappropriate from another. That may cause you to have guilt about your reaction.

The symptoms of an escalating boundary issue may elude you completely. You may have blind spots to some kinds of boundary issues. You don't hear someone being disrespectful until it is so blatant that you would have to be blind and dumb not to be aware of it. Why were you unaware of the intensifying symptoms of someone being disrespectful?

Do not be too hard on yourself if you have missed the symptoms. We are all products of our life experience. Like the horse which becomes numb from a rider who kicks too much, you have become numb to certain kinds of disrespectful behavior. Only when the kick is directed at your stomach do you become aware that this person may have been abusing you all along.

Boundary issues are often issues because you have unknowingly allowed yourself to be too available. You may be so nice that a bully looking for a target sees you as weak. You may work hard at relationships and as a result have attracted individuals who expect you to do all the work. You may have such low expectations of how you will be treated that you accept behaviors that others might not. There may be some reason that you are so grateful for a person's attention that you allow that person to take advantage of your good will. You may feel dependent on that person's actions for some reason and so you do not react to symptoms that the person is not treating you with respect.

There are so many reasons that you might allow others to invade or abuse your comfort zone. Unfortunately, many of us are not conscious of those reasons or our distorted behaviors until we can no longer ignore the effect.

Examples of Potential Issues

When a person attempts to be helpful and you have a negative reaction, ask yourself if you are reacting because you have a sense that the person is attempting to create a situation where you will owe him or her.

When someone seems to have inappropriate timing, you may want to ask yourself whether you are simply too sensitive or whether there is a problem brewing. It becomes a problem when you feel as though you have no privacy or free time because the other person consistently invades it.

The perpetrator often camouflages a boundary issue with specific objectives, desires, intentions. An example might be a call to your home at 10 pm suggesting that the person needs something immediately. You may have a boundary issue if the person does this frequently for things that could wait.

Other kinds of boundary issues might feel like intrusions into your privacy. These could include asking inappropriate questions or telling inappropriate stories about you to others. These are attempts to dominate and should be seen as such. The Buster may be attempting to dominate you or, if the story is *about* you to others, he or she may be trying to dominate the other party by being the one in the "know." The symptom is the way you feel about the interaction.

If you feel that the Boundary Buster's questions are intrusive, and yet circumstance makes you feel compelled to answer, you are in a Power Game. The person is using something about his or her Positional Power to manipulate you into sharing information you would rather not share.

There are also boundary issues around personal space. We have space boundaries that are unique to our own preferences. Some of us are comfortable in close proximity to others and some of us are not. And we are often comfortable close to some people and not to others.

There are people who use space as a form of Power Game. He or she might get close to your face in order to communicate more forcefully. This is an attempt to dominate through intimidation. It is a destructive attempt to communicate. This same person might ignore doors and knocking as a form of asking permission to enter your space.

Should You Be Reacting?

You may not care. Then it is not a boundary issue. It becomes a boundary issue when you *feel* something negative as a result of his or her behavior. It may be subtle and that may cause you to overlook what is happening or to feel as though to respond would be inappropriate.

If you feel a negative response and you do nothing, you are caught in the "being nice" syndrome. They may be invading your space but it would seem impolite for you to call them on it.

There is another particularly difficult kind of Boundary Buster because of its subtlety. This is the HELPFUL Boundary Power Gamer. In this case, think of the boundary issue as a kind of false helpfulness where the desire is not so much to help you, but to control you. What makes it confusing is that it is offered in a way that appears as though the person only has your interest at heart. You become puzzled because you think you should be grateful but you don't feel grateful. You feel anxious, annoyed, angry. Trust yourself enough to explore why you feel that way.

Destructive Impulses From Those Who Care?

One of the tactics the HELPFUL boundary abuser might use is to involve him or her self in your life and the decisions you make. This person looks for ways to control you by giving advice. Because the person makes a point of showing you what you do not understand about people and events in your life, you feel weak and stupid whenever he or she is around.

Not all helpful advisors are intruding on your boundaries. The clues are in how the person interacts with you. If the person cannot acknowledge your strengths, does not seem to value you, and only seems happy when he or she is finding fault, you may want to examine the relationship and you may want to move him or her out of your life.

If you have to be weak for this person to feel good about him or her self, this person may be robbing you of your self-esteem. Scott Peck wrote a book about this kind of Power Game called *The People of the Lie*. If you remember the movie *The Dead Poets' Society,* the parents used this technique to control their son, who ultimately committed suicide.

In the movie *Postcards from the Edge*, Shirley Maclane constantly reminds her daughter, Meryl Streep, that she, the mother, is superior. No matter what the daughter does, she is reminded that she is brainless, and not good enough by her mother. There is an ongoing dialogue about the foolishness of the decisions the daughter has made. The interaction is not supportive or loving, in spite of the constant proclamations from the mother of how much she loves her daughter.

Worst Case!

In some circumstances, not having clarity around your boundaries and your own understanding of them, may have disastrous consequences. In *The Gift of Fear* Gavin de Becker discusses the serious results of not listening to your own warning bells regarding people who are abusing your boundaries.

The book is written by a retired law enforcement official and the content is about violent crime. Often the victim allows boundary invasions, many of them simple, before the attack. The problem is that many people do not know how to trust themselves in evaluating what is appropriate and what is not. Niceness takes over where firmly repelling the invader over fundamental boundary invasions could have saved them years of grief.

Some Common Boundary Invasions

The list below refers to behaviors that may indicate boundary Power Games. It is difficult to rank them in terms of seriousness because the circumstance and the number of repetitions of the behavior may escalate the consequences of the issue. You may be in a Power Game for dominance with boundary issues if a person you know is doing any or all of the following things:

Suspicious behaviors:

- refusing to take "no" for an answer
- showing up uninvited
- trying to get you to do things through guilt (probably deserves its own chapter)
- attempting to use gifts or entertainment as a way of making you his or her friend

- talking about you to others as if they are intimately involved in your life (when they are not)
- talking to you as if you are intimately involved in his or her life when you are not, and have no desire to be
- frequently calling at times that you would normally choose not to be available (late in the evening or early morning)
- saying inappropriate things to you or about you
- physically moving in too close in a way that feels disrespectful
- interrupting you either physically or verbally or both
- standing way too close when they are talking to you for your comfort
- acting like a victim whom you are *supposed* to save (guilt).

All of the behaviors in the list above, in the right circumstance, may be a Power Game about boundaries. Your boundaries. You are the one who should set those boundaries. It takes a lot of knowledge of self to know how to deal appropriately with Power Games where someone is using boundaries to control you.

Do Others Take You for a Fool?

Another form of boundary issues is when others take advantage of your generosity. If you can identify a pattern of abuse where others whom you believe you have treated well have taken advantage of you, you will want to understand that there may be many moments where you were simply too nice. Some examples of being too nice might be the following:

- allowing others to borrow your things without question.

- giving access to private information without reserve.
- being available without indicating your own needs.
- paying generously for all services without expecting and demanding respect and fairness in return.

You may be to worried about being fair, being liked or sending any message of mistrust or distrust. In other words, you have set yourself to look like someone who deserves to be taken advantage of. What a shame. You then look and feel like a victim when you were coming from some motive that might have been about treating others as you wanted to be treated.

Remember, real Leadership is *never* naive. If you are surprised by others taking advantage of your boundaries, you are probably naive. Do not feel too bad. Over time you will become less so.

Analysis

If you know yourself well enough to know that you are frequently a victim of other people abusing your boundaries, you may want to go back to basics. What is it that you believe about how the world works that is causing you to be a victim? Get some help if this has become a serious issue for you.

If you have attempted to assert your boundaries and it has not worked, an analysis using Vector Analysis is an important first step to gaining an understanding of the root issues underlying Power Games around your boundaries.

Analysis is done to identify how you opened the door to the Game, as well as to clarify the points on which you might focus to end the Game.

The analysis has two levels. The first level is to work through a sequence of questions on Personal and Positional Power (in Appendix A). The questions will help you to identify problem areas where you have lower scores. You may even want to graph your results. The second level of analysis is to identify your perceived risk in the situation.

Analyzing properly takes total honesty. It can be a painful process to discover your weaknesses as well as to recognize the consequences of those weaknesses. Too often, it is easier to blame the opponent for their "dirty" tactics. Unfortunately, if left unchecked, the weakness may act as a magnet to bring the Game back to you again and again. Even if your worst nemesis is removed, he or she will in all likelihood reoccur in another form until you deal with your own problems.

Here's How it Works

Suppose you have what you think may be a boundary issue. To identify your x and y values, you should answer the questions located in Appendix A on yourself regarding the circumstance about which you are concerned.

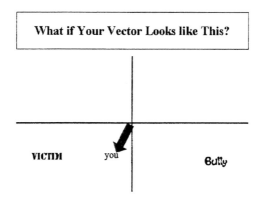

57

You know that you want to move the *resulting* vector (the one you get by combining your vector with your adversary's) into the first quadrant where Leadership is the outcome. You may have a long way to go, particularly if he is a true bully.

If Your Adversary is a Bully

Assume that you cannot change him. You will need to exert a big enough change on *you* to pull the whole outcome into the first quadrant. At the moment, the outcome is down in the Bully quadrant at the corner of the completed parallelogram.

How do you exert such a change? You will have to change both your Positional Power and your Personal Power enough to get your arrow into the first quadrant where Leaders hang out.

Where Should You Focus?

People who do not have a lot of trouble with boundary issues are set up differently than those who do. If you are someone who attracts boundary issues, you may have to push a reset button by changing

58

some of your attitudes regarding the *Suspicious Behaviors* listed in the previous section.

After you have an idea of where the problems may be, the second part of the analysis (risk assessment) becomes relevant. You are not responding correctly because you have some real or perceived risk regarding the situation of which you may not even be aware.

The questions regarding Positional and Personal Power in the Appendix should help you to get clear as to which aspects of that risk are contorting your behavior in a way that keeps the bully coming. After you have identified your weak areas, you are only partially finished with assessment.

You should next assess three things.

1.   *What* are the consequences you fear?
2.   *How Likely* are the consequences you fear?
3.   **What are the *actual* consequences you are facing as a result of *not* dealing effectively with the situation, and how do they stack up next to your fear?**

Managing Boundaries Effectively

Once you know your low scores on x and y and what it is specifically that you fear, you may want to examine your thinking or your beliefs around those areas of concern which emerge from your analysis. Here are some potential examples in which adjusting your beliefs may change your response in a way that will probably cause alternative results:

1.   If people are abusing you or your boundaries, your need to be *nice* may need to be replaced with a need to be *clear* as a higher priority.
2.   If you have a great need for approval, it may distort your sense of what you deserve.
3.   You may be allowing personal security to outweigh your *dignity* in how you set your priorities. You may think you are saying "no", but pay attention to what you *do*. If you fear peers or bosses, you may be allowing boundary invasions because you are worried about your job. Areas for concern regarding this point:
      •   Bosses *do not* outrank you in all aspects of your life. They only outrank you in your job!
      •   Harassment is not a part of any job description.
3.   You may not understand what is expected of you when you make a commitment. As a result, you set yourself up to feel betrayed or disappointed when others make demands that interfere with your plans. It may be your inability to ask the right questions or to stay clear about what you are agreeing to that causes you to feel as though others are invading your boundaries when they begin demanding your attention.
4.   You may have an unclear vision for you and how you live your life. If so, you may react to what you believe is inevitable rather than assert your will. (If you are destroying your self-esteem in order to keep a job you hate, a spouse who abuses you, a friend who is at best a lousy friend, you are probably not keeping the long term agenda in mind. The long term agenda is ultimately about how you want to live your life.)
5.   You may believe that others have control of your life. If you believe that, you may be inclined to make decisions which allow them to abuse your boundaries.
6.   You may believe that you have to justify your feelings when you feel that someone is invading your boundaries. This may

cause you to be less effective in simply asking a person to stop doing whatever it is they are doing. You do not have to justify your feelings to anyone. They are yours.

7. It is generally true that if a bullying individual feels that you will not protect your boundaries, the situation may escalate. You may want to get feedback from others you trust about you and whether you are inadvertently sending others a message that you will allow some kinds of abuse of boundaries.

Technique

These are some things you might try for effect when dealing with Boundary issues, not necessarily in this order:

- Just say "no"!
- Say "no thank you."
- Leave; do not stay in the presence of the person pushing on your boundary.
- Whining is not allowed! You are not a child attempting to get your way by making others feel sorry for you!
- Try telling them to stop doing what they are doing because you do not like it. Directly. Do not be tempted to put it in a note or an e-mail. Those are symptoms of your fear of confrontation.
- Suggest an alternative behavior; bosses who call at home at all hours might be convinced to use e-mail (unlikely if you do not tell them that you are bothered by his or her invasion of your private time before you make the suggestion.)
- For those who would like to run your life, provide no access. Stop telling them your plans, especially if they do not handle information with respect. This is often the only way to get family members to stop trying to control you; painful but effective.

■   For those who use guilt to control you, let go of whatever you
    fear their retaliation will be. If someone would manipulate you
    through guilt, they do not deserve your loyalty.

Things to Remember:

1. **Never assume that rank is the definitive Positional Power.
    They do not *own* you because they outrank you *unless* you
    believe they do.**
2. **Tone is key. People who *believe* that they have the right to
    protect themselves usually do. When they say "no", the
    other person hears "no". Do your attackers hear "no"
    when you say "no"?**
3. **You may find a solution that addresses both your needs
    and the abuser's. This does not mean a solution that the
    abuser will love.**
4. **Examine your beliefs around the circumstance you are
    dealing with. Contained within those beliefs may be the
    reasons why you are abused and others are not.**
5. **Humor can be a powerful way of handling a boundary
    issue that is beginning to surface. It is less effective with
    more established patterns.**

Ten

Harassment
The Worst Kind of Boundary Issue

Definition of Harassment

Harassment takes many forms. It can be as simple as pestering and as complicated and diabolical as inappropriate sexual behavior (the ultimate Power Game). Harassment is done to create a reaction from *you*. The perpetrator is only satisfied when he or she gets a response. It is, as are all Power Games, an attempt to assert dominance. What makes it harassment is what you *feel* about the interactions with this person. An assault on your boundaries (physical or emotional) once or twice is an invasion. When you feel besieged or stalked, it is harassment.

The attacker is getting pleasure from your discomfort. It reinforces his or her sense of Positional Power if you are frightened, frustrated or stressed because of the behavior. The more powerless or victimized you are, the more satisfaction for the offender. They have chosen a type of behavior which they know is particularly offensive to you personally. They are looking for a reaction and you are probably giving it to them.

Sadly, sometimes they are simply looking for attention and do not know how to get it in a reasonable and healthy way. And so, they find a behavior that is likely to give them what they want.

Symptoms of Harassment

Most people know when they are being harassed. They feel as though the behavior, in whatever way it manifests, is **repetitive** and **relentless.** There is little if any relief, and although there may be time gaps in the behavior, there is the feeling that the perpetrator (or perpetrators) is lurking and waiting for the right moment to invade your boundary again. You never relax because you are convinced that as soon as you do, you will be attacked again.

The difference between harassment and other forms of boundary issues may be mostly in the degree of the invasion and in the intent. A person who is annoying because they seem to have missed adulthood 101 in their understanding of appropriate behavior is not necessarily harassing you.

If you are increasingly worried or stressed by the behavior or if your feeling is one of fear, you are dealing with a serious boundary issue which is likely to escalate. Trust yourself. If you feel fear, you are not overreacting.

Note: in this text, we are referring to the kind of harassment that may take place in the work environment that is more than annoying, and possibly job threatening. If for any reason you feel *physically* unsafe or threatened, you should seek professional and possibly police involvement. Harassment that involves physical threat is beyond the focus of the content of this text.

Analysis

You should want to understand specifically why *you* are the target.

You may be too weak on the establishment of your boundaries. Answer all of the questions from Positional and Personal Power in the Appendix A to determine if *you* have created doubt in this person's mind about your ability to protect yourself.

Be very clear in your evaluation of yourself. Do not sugar coat your own weaknesses. The cost to you is already too great. Acknowledge your fear regarding the person or circumstance and also acknowledge your own ability(or inability) to be strong and clear with this person and possibly, in general.

Your analysis should include both the determination of your vector coordinates by asking the questions about *you* from Appendix A, and then a risk assessment to find out what you fear. You will find an in-depth assessment of a true sexual harassment case study in our workbook.

Management of Harassment

The first thing to remember in terms of resolution is that you should try not to do anything out of Powerlessness. Move slowly and carefully as you decide what you will do to stop the behavior. The sequence of steps you take may make the difference between success and embroiling yourself deeper in a very distressing circumstance.

You should know and understand the domino effect of each action before you take it. For example, knowing the culture in your organization is critical for finding the correct response. There are cultures which have low tolerance for harassing behavior, zero

65

tolerance for sexual harassment, and have systems in place to deal with the behaviors definitively. Be careful not to assume, however, that the systems themselves will assure you a quick and helpful response. The systems may be in place, but the actual culture of the organization may still be into "shooting the messenger."

Study the culture itself. Many cultures have established Human Resource avenues for dealing with abuse but have a reputation of dealing harshly with the person who files the complaint.

The person who is harassing you is also important. What is his or her reputation? Has he or she gotten away with bad behavior in the past? Why? What is his or her network and how does it stack up against yours? What is his or her Positional Power status and how might it be used in his or her favor?

Don't be offended by the above questions. They are a means for clarifying the Power Game and for determining the correct response. Do not visit more problems on yourself by your choices.

Always Work From Personal Power

First, when seeking and taking advice, be sure that you are going to someone whom you respect for his or her *wisdom*. There are too many individuals who will advise you to do something when they have no understanding or concern for the consequences you may reap.

Don't be naive by assuming that your HR representative will know exactly the right moves. This person may know the law, but they may not understand the culture any better than you do. Your HR representative may also be quick to recommend the formal system because he or she believes in it, but may be as surprised as you when the organization responds badly to such a move.

Second, determine the *criteria* for any solution. Be clear that you are *not* trying to get even or hurt the other person as a solution. Hurting him or her is not a solution. It is a response. You may feel entitled to do so but you are looking for *resolution*, not vengeance. Try to remember that the other person is playing by street rules and if you engage in street rules, you will probably lose. Any move to hurt the person is likely to result in a reaction that hurts you more. Think in terms of the Power Graph and the placement of your vector if you were to choose a solution of revenge.

Criteria for appropriate solutions might include: 1)action causes behavior to stop, 2)action causes person to respect you, 3)action causes person to feel bad about his or her behavior and *want* to change, 4)action causes organization to learn and grow from the choice you make. (See New Rules for Power Games in Chapter 6.)

When you are deciding if a response is the correct response, ask if it meets any or all of the above criteria and be suspicious of a solution which does not. Causing the person pain, shame, grief, money, time etc, might make you feel better, but it invites further attack and may be damaging to the organization. What you do not know is how far the other person is willing to go to win. Engaging in a solution of revenge or punishment may be far more destructive than you can even imagine.

Third, pay attention to *cause and effect*. If what you do escalates the problem, figure out why. Try something else.

Be careful and concerned about any move that is an attempt to assert or bring Positional Power into play to stop the problem. Filing a harassment complaint is an attempt to exert the Positional Power of the organization on the perpetrator to stop the problem. It is also, often an attempt to hurt the other person due to your own sense of powerlessness. Often the backlash from such a move is both surprising and devastating.

What would a Personal Power response look like? It will depend specifically on the circumstance. What you are attempting to do is look at the situation and objectively ask the question, "What is the response which will give me the best outcome for me *and* for the organization?"

Let's look at some possible steps that may diffuse the situation rather than escalate it.

Examples of Some Responses to Different Forms of Harassment

With harassment, the confrontation is usually better if it is sooner, rather than later. Harassment gets worse if you do not put a stop to it immediately. Here are some techniques that have been tried successfully in the professional environment:

NOTE: Anything you say should be said with confidence. If you speak from fear or anger, you will diminish the impact of your response. Also, the overriding rule is to handle these issues with GRACE. Be careful of any response which sounds common or crude. That will throw you into the same culture as your attacker which will definitely NOT make the organization a better place. Moving slowly and deliberately is wise. Freezing is different. Remember that much of communication is subliminal. If you freeze out of fear, your attacker will probably know that it is fear rather than deliberation which is causing your response.

Ongoing, Inappropriate Comments

1. In response to inappropriate comments: you might say, "Excuse me, I'm sure that I did not hear you clearly. Would you please repeat that?"

    Rationale: Often bullies are simply reacting. To ask them to repeat themselves often stops them cold. Even the bully is aware of how bad it sounds the second time around.

2. Another direct response is to identify what you are feeling and why. The attacker may find that such a response causes him or her to rethink motives. For example: "I am certain that you did not mean to do so, but that comment felt very demeaning."

    Rationale: Even if he or she *did* mean to demean you, very few people are meanspirited enough to like the fact that they have acted deliberately in a way that is demeaning. They have given themselves permission to act mean either through habit or as a response to some perceived weakness in you which "justifies" the behavior. When you call it for what it is, calmly and respectfully ("I'm sure you did not mean to do so,..."), they are sometimes left feeling their own sense of shame for what they have done and how they have made you feel.

What if You Let it Go Too Far?

3. What if the behavior has gone on for a while and has *escalated* over time? If you wait, these behaviors get harder to stop, so again, we recommend that you catch it early and clearly. If you did not stop it early, however, your response may need to acknowledge that you should have responded sooner. For example: "I should have told you earlier how much I dislike it

when you ..... I know you would not do it if you understood how it makes me feel."

Rationale: You are stating a boundary. And yet, once again, you are attempting to "make the Right things easy" for this person. By assuming that he or she does not want to make you feel this way, you give him or her an opportunity to step back and consider if he or she likes the idea of *deliberately*, repetitively, doing something that makes you feel bad.

Yes, they have already made this choice, but now you force the person to make the choice *consciously*. Often, bad behavior is unconscious and when you make it conscious, you change the dynamic. Also, be prepared to LISTEN. You may find that he or she has some of his or her own complaints about how you have made him or her feel. *Listening* to your enemy is a choice to come from Personal Power.

4. Suppose this is a really bad person who continues even after you have given them every opportunity to stop. Now you become more forceful with your response. Remember, come from confidence, not fear. "This is unprofessional and unacceptable. It will stop or you might consider how it will sound if I am forced to talk to others about what you are doing."

This may be the moment when the Bully attempts to make you feel like a fool for overreacting. ***Don't*** go into an argument about whether or not you are overreacting. That is an endless cycle and takes you nowhere. You do not have to justify your preferences. You simply have to make them clear.

70

"It is irrelevant to me whether you think I am overreacting or not. I find your comments/behavior offensive." Classy and clear.

Are You Part of the Problem?

5.   When someone does not stop after you have repeatedly asked them to discontinue a behavior, ask yourself if you have been really clear. If there is any reason that the person might have thought you were being playful or did not mean it, then you may need to understand that. Ask someone you trust if they think the message was clear. If you have no doubt that this person is continuing after understanding that you would like them to stop, then you need to confront them in a different way than you have in the past. (If what you are doing is not working, don't do more of it.)

Response: this might be the moment to bring your boss into the situation if it is professional. Do *not* ask your boss to take over. Set up a meeting with you, the boss and the offender. You may want to be there to keep the other person accountable to telling the truth. Otherwise, you have no idea what he or she may tell your boss and you will have no way of defending yourself. Bullies are often capable of stretching the story, accusing you of initiating the behavior, etc.. Having the boss intervene without being there is also a cop out. You are hoping someone will deal with your problem. Stay with it until it is over. You may learn something about you that you need to learn as well.

6.   What if it is your boss who seems to take pleasure in humiliating you? He or she often makes fun of your contributions in front of the team. Perhaps your boss has a wicked and biting sense of humor and because he or she holds

the Positional Power, your boss often gets laughs for the comments to you or about you even though they are demeaning and sarcastic.

Response: Analysis is key here. What is it about you which makes you so vulnerable to attempts at humor at your expense? You may want to go through the questions on Personal Power very carefully and find the weaknesses. Your boss is unquestionably a "piece of work", but you may miss the benefit from this situation if you do not identify your weakness before you respond. There is always a "cause and effect" relationship behind this kind of behavior. Your boss lacks boundaries and you have not done a good job of setting them.

The correct response is always specific to the circumstance. Understanding your boss and his or her motives may affect the response. There are some general rules for starting the intervention.

For example, your response to his or her behavior should be private. You should set an appointment with your boss.

Secondly, you should start from an assumption that he or she would rather be a good boss than not. (This is difficult but critical to a successful outcome.)

A conversation with your boss should include helping him or her to understand your response to his or her behavior and then some very careful and intense listening.

Example: "I know that you are concerned with my performance. I am having a hard time focusing on how to fix it because when I speak or prepare to speak during our meetings, I dread having my peers laugh at me. You have such a quick sense of humor and I envy that, but I don't know if you know how it affects me."

"I really would like to understand two things. What will it take to make you happy with my work, and how can I get comfortable with presenting in front of you and my peers. Right now I feel as though I am in a downward spiral because my anticipation of what is going to occur is making it hard to think clearly and I suspect that I am just making it worse."

Next, you should prepare to listen with an intention to figure out what *you* might be doing wrong. Your boss does not like you for some reason and you need to know what it is.

Rational: By making it your problem and assuming that your boss really does not understand how it affects you, you also assumes that he or she really wants to be a good boss. (This is "making the right things easy.") Your boss is given the opportunity to talk to you about what is causing him or her to respond this way to you.

It is important to remember that the outcome you want is to make it easy for your boss to want to treat you better. That is less likely if you attack or accuse him or her of being a bad boss. It is almost impossible to create a better outcome if you simply grumble about your boss to others. If you listen openly to your boss and stay curious, you give him or her the opportunity to tell you what he or she has obviously been uncomfortable telling you.

There is something about you that causes your boss to be a bully and if you find out what it is you have a chance to correct it even as you are causing him or her to be accountable for the effect of his or her behavior.

Note: your boss may be a bully in his or her nature. That is irrelevant to you. You want to understand why your boss is bullying *you*. It is unlikely that your boss will bully every single person with whom he or she comes into contact. Give him or her a chance to identify what you do that brings out the worst in his or her behavior.

Summary

The above examples are meant to offer options only. Clearly, every situation is unique and you may need to assess your situation to determine a course of action. The thing to remember is that you want to fix it, not have revenge. If you go for revenge instead of fixing the situation, you are highly likely to escalate a bad situation. Do so at your own risk.

Check to be sure that you are not feeling righteous. Such an attitude may cause you to do things which may invite more attack. That is what you don't want. You want peace. You want to be left alone. You will probably get your best result if you can detach from judgment and attempt to deal with the situation objectively.

You may find better ways to handle a person who is harassing you. Many people think they have done the things suggested above, but tone makes a dramatic difference. If you sound like a victim, your attacker will probably assume you are powerless. If you sound serious, and clear from the beginning, unless they have a career death wish, they will probably back off.

Things to Remember:

1. Do not freeze when you are treated inappropriately. Identify what you are feeling and why, and then think through what you should do to stop the behavior.
2. Do not become emotional. If you do, get control of yourself before you respond.
3. If you ask for assistance, be sure that you are not doing so as a victim who cannot take care of yourself. Only involve those whom you respect as being wise. Otherwise you may complicate a difficult situation and you may be the victim of their lack of wisdom.
4. Hurting the other person to get your way is discouraged. It will not pull you into the leadership quadrant and often opens new Power Games.
5. Ask the question you do not want to know the answer to. "What is it about me that is causing you to behave in this way?" This may just be a bully who bullies everyone, but if you get an answer, it may help you to understand how not to attract bullies, regardless of what a bad egg the other person is.

Eleven

Corporate Cutthroat

Definition of Corporate Cutthroat

Corporate Cutthroat is a form of Power Game in which the victim is often the person who tries to think of what is best for the organization. Because victims of Corporate Cutthroat work so hard for the organization, they are often surprised with the viciousness of the attacks.

There is a purpose behind Corporate Cutthroat. It is usually accompanied by attempts to grab power (or turf), malicious attempts to disparage the other person, public aggressiveness, and bullying. The issue is ultimately about control.

Corporate Cutthroat may be different than other games about boundaries because the victim has usually given the attacker a reason to fear him or her.

Perhaps the victim of the attack has favor with someone of importance. Often he or she is visibly more talented. Our victim may have a better handle on the business than the attacker. The attacker is often incompetent, unconscious of that fact (attackers in Corporate Cutthroat often have delusions about their competence) and is attempting to divert attention from his or her lack of true direction.

Why so harsh a view of the attacker? Have you ever seen a really secure, confident person attack the security or livelihood of another? They simply do not do it. If there is an attack going on, there is probably insecurity behind it.

The aggression serves as a means to make the victim look ineffective, and has the added result of drawing others into the chaos by forcing them to take sides. At a *subliminal* level, the person attacking, knows that he or she is in over his or her head, but is incapable of acknowledging that fact. The attacks buy both control and time, with the ultimate objective often being to ride the roller coaster for long enough to cash out.

Sometimes, the aggressor has an even more important reason to attack. He or she is involved in questionable practices (legal or ethical). The hostility serves as intimidation. If the victim is intimidated, he or she might be less likely to take on the issue. Remember, the attacker only needs to last long enough to take his or her spoils and leave.

If you have a peer or subordinate who seems to be deliberately attempting to destroy you, you are very probably involved in the Game of Corporate Cutthroat. Trust that he or she has a reason for attacking *you*, as opposed to others, and usually it is about something real that he or she is trying to hide.

Symptoms of Corporate Cutthroat

If you feel as though someone is singling you out for attack, you are probably right. If it feels as though the offensive is escalating, it probably is. If you feel as though the attacker is trying to wear you down until you leave, you may be correct.

Initially, the attacker may be subtle. He or she will probably cover up his or her intention and bad behavior in front of others, at least with those others who might be capable of defending you. Your attacker will set you up again and again to look like you are not communicating, not responding to his or her requests, or not trying to work with him or her.

You will undoubtably play right into his or her hands. You may "lose it" because of the unfairness of the accusations. You will probably *not* be calm and objective, but instead reactive, angry, and closed. Attackers often successfully make their victims so angry that the victim appears to be losing control. Your opponent may in comparison, be calm, rational, and may have twisted responses on your part to make it look like you are overemotional.

Unfortunately, the angrier and more self-righteous you are, the worse you will look. It won't matter if you are right. You may be completely dismayed and amazed that others cannot seem to see what is happening.

Over time, the behaviors will probably become more open. This is usually after your attacker senses that you are losing ground in the organization. He or she may begin to make overt grabs for your territory, your resources, or your subordinates, and he or she will probably expect to win, because after all, you are obviously overwhelmed.

Those you expect to defend you may back down. You may wonder how they can be so weak.

You should not wonder. While it seems that others are oblivious to what is happening, they are not oblivious at all. They simply do not want to be the next victim of this particular kind of terrorist. Even bosses become cautious in taking on this person. They hope you may simply back down and learn to get along. Because your behavior also appears to be out of control, to take sides with you may in fact jeopardize the boss's credibility with the rest of the team.

Analysis

When you have individuals in key Leadership positions engaging in Power Games it may be very destructive. Look at the graphs below. Individuals working against each other in Cutthroat Games create an outcome (in other words, a culture) that is about bullying. Even if you act as a Leader, look where the outcome falls.

A Leader and a Bully Interact

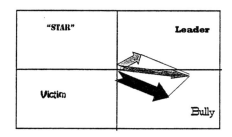

Victims of Corporate Cutthroat are not your Victim type!

The victim in these scenarios is not usually the victim type at all. The victims in Corporate Cutthroat usually think of themselves as strong people, with strong characters. They usually are. Unfortunately, Corporate Cutthroat is a case of one person playing by a different set of rules than the other. The frustration and rage the person feels often turn this normally strong person into a victim. Their impotence in the face of someone not playing fair often makes the result even worse.

If you handle it really badly and
turn into a victim?

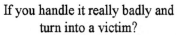

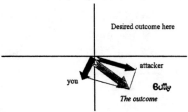

If you think of yourself as a normally very strong individual, it may be harder for you to answer the questions around Personal and Positional Power based on what is *actually happening* as opposed to what you believe *should* be happening.

You may struggle with questions like, "establishes appropriate boundaries." You might think you do. The law of cause and effect says you do *not*, at least with this particular person. Why is that? You are getting an "effect" which is that a person is seriously abusing your boundaries. There is always a set of events which lead up to Corporate Cutthroat. You were a participant in those events. Can you be realistic enough to identify your own causal behaviors in those events?

When you are in a rage, it is hard for you to listen, it is difficult to appropriately establish boundaries, and impossible to recognize that your anger is actually working against you. People become ineffectual because of their state of mind. You may listen badly, react poorly, and otherwise move your status from leader to victim. The longer it goes on, the worse shape you are in. To improve the situation, whether you are leader or victim, you may have to do all the work. The other person will probably remain a bully.

80

When you raise your Personal Power, the result is dragged into the Leadership quadrant regardless of what your opponent chooses to do. Others will learn more from your behavior as you raise your Personal Power. Raising your Personal Power is the best way to create a better outcome for the whole even if your opponent does not change at all.

Suppose you start as a victim and then work to raise your y coordinate by increasing your Personal Power. Your opponent does not change. Look at the change in the outcome in this scenario as you raise y without affecting your Positional Power and without your opponent changing at all.

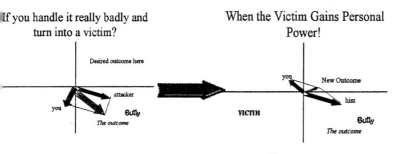

Learn the Lessons

As you can see in both scenarios above, when you raise your *y* coordinate by becoming clearer and focusing on your Personal Power, it *does* make a difference to the organization. It may not look like much but if it raises the outcome from Bully quadrant to Leadership quadrant, it means that the organization is now positioned better than it was when you were a total victim.

Many victims of Corporate Cutthroat get to the point that they would rather leave the organization than put up with the garbage. They lose

81

faith in the organization, begin talking to the headhunters, and our attacker wins. Unfortunately, our victim often gains little from opting out of the Game. He or she has learned nothing and will probably run into others with the mentality of our attacker *over and over again.*

A new attacker will probably find our victim in new locations and the dance may begin again and again until the victim learns how to play. Ultimately, many fine leaders never develop to the point that they can actually reap the rewards of their talents because they do not learn to take on this Bully personality.

Taking on the Bully by raising your Personal Power isn't easy, but it is a right of passage to the tops of most organizations. Is it any wonder that we have so many unethical, poor decision-makers at the top? Few of the really fine people working their way up the food chain have the stomach to get through this inevitable Game.

Managing Corporate Cutthroat Effectively

Decide that you are going to tough it out. That is the first step. And then, decide that you are going to be clever about how you begin to Play. Clever is very important. You can still play by the Rules outlined in Chapter Six and work toward the good of the organization. The difference is that you are going to adapt a strategy for your own behavior that has the potential to clarify who the Leaders and Bullies really are.

There are some general recommendations for how to handle this battle if you want to win it.

First, you need to stay calm.

Second, stop being surprised at how low the other person may go. Anticipate it. This person is playing for big stakes, your job. You must not be naive about what *should be* vs what is!

Next, be prepared to get tough. You may need to be tougher in order to win. You do not stoop to their rules. That would work against the organization. You take the high road, but you do so realistically.

How Does Cutthroat Work?

First: Bullies Divert Attention from the Move They Are Making.

The bully is going to attempt to divert attention from any issues you raise. Period. You may never be able to anticipate *how* he or she is going to do this, but you should anticipate that he or she probably will. Stop being sucked in. It is one of the main things that make you a victim.

You are very likely trying to be rational and argue against the logic of what he is presenting. Logic was never his plan. Diversion was his plan. The minute you engage in an argument with him, he wins. The argument itself takes precedent and becomes the diversion he was seeking. The more blatantly *emotional* the argument becomes, the more effective he has been. He is very likely to call you stupid, irrational, soft, irrelevant, etc.

Instead of responding or engaging, find a quiet place and ask yourself, "what is the main concern I have about what he is attempting to do?" Is it legal a legal issue, is it an ethical issue, is it efficiency? Is the bully attempting to do something that you believe will cause morale issues? There are so many violations of good leadership by this individual. Whatever it is, you should define yourself around the *issue*, not around the flak he may send up.

Example

For example: Our Bully is playing Corporate Cutthroat where he attempts to minimize the efforts of others and maximize his own result at their expense. In this case, the bully wants to "strong arm" the members of your distribution network of your product to do something that is clearly against their best interests in order to make his numbers look better. You start to indicate that you think that this is a bad business decision, and the next thing you know, you are in the middle of an argument about how soft you are and how "good business" is about being tough.

You feel that he is being ridiculous and try to present evidence that good business is good relationships. Soon the discussion is about how emotional you are being and if you cannot be practical, perhaps you should not be in a position of leadership.

You just got sucked in. It was never about you. It was about your distributors. When you respond to his jabs, you simply say, "I may be soft, but what you are suggesting is a good way to turn our most valuable asset into an enemy." You never divert to a dissection of your style, or good business vs bad business, or whatever he throws out, even though it is very seductive. Remember, these guys have been practicing their techniques for a while.

Second: Bullies Playing Cutthroat Want to Place You at Odds with Your Allies

The bully may attempt to place you at odds with others who might otherwise be your allies. Particular targets are bosses. Here's the trap. You expect your boss to see this blatant attempt to engage the organization in bad practices or ideas. You are amazed and disappointed in your boss's lack of leadership in taking on the bully.

84

Soon, you are disgusted with your boss and the relationship deteriorates. Strong individuals quickly lose patience with bosses who do not stand up for what is right.

In the background, our friend is telling the boss how much he admires you, how much he would like to work with you and how hard he is trying. You appear emotional and out of control and your boss hesitates to get in the middle because he cannot defend your reactions. Your reactions are more than a little intense and you are not pretending to try to get along, or like this guy. You are quite clearly responding to a JERK.

You are putting the boss in a position where all he or she wants to do is have this 'thing' between you two disappear. He or she becomes even more absent. You become more disgusted with your boss and, since Poker was not your game, you show it. Guess who is the Bully now?

Third: You Begin to Disengage

When you start talking to the headhunters, people know. You become expendable. You have declared that you are no longer a part of a team. You tried, but others may not see that. All they see is you and the fact that you are not even attempting to get along. You are emotional, often weepy or angry, and just plain tough to be around. You lose. People know the other guy is an idiot, but you have disappointed them as well.

What Should You Do?

You want to fix this? Here is what you have to do. Get some distance from the issues you believe in. They are chits on a board, not life or death. Let go of the crusade--not the issues--the *crusade*. Righteous behavior will probably not help you win. Win is the objective. Win is moving the ball toward the organizational win. It is *not* about *every* play, it is about the direction.

You state your position and back off. You stop engaging in the skirmishes. Our friend may not know how to handle that. If you are good enough at stating your opinion without all the emotion, what you have done is make it clear to those moving the ball that they have *chosen* to move the ball in the wrong direction. "I cannot support that action because I believe that it will be detrimental to the organization. If you choose to support it, it will be over my stated objections."

If that is too strong and you believe that it makes you a "non team player" say the same thing more elegantly. But, you still need to be clear. You might choose for example to say, "I hope we are keeping the needs of the customer in mind. That solution feels like it needs a little more work in order to reflect that bias clearly."

You stop attempting to exert your will and instead assert your belief. This is a big distinction. You allow the others to assume their adult responsibility for making mistakes, even big mistakes, instead of trying to pull them the other direction. Keep in mind that if they are not listening to your point of view anyway, a calm statement is more effective in the debrief after their mistake is apparent. A disagreeable, argumentative person will simply be viewed as part of the problem after the facts become apparent.

They have already told you they would rather take the easy way. You have little to lose by allowing them to learn some tough lessons. (If the cutthroat continues, you will be moving on at some point anyway). If you are clear, and not embattled, you may stand out as the voice of dissension after the dust settles. If you are embroiled in turf wars, you may even get blamed.

State your opinion and then keep quiet (unless of course, fighting is working). Allow nature to take over. This may go against your instincts completely. You are into control or you would not be in this battle. You are not used to allowing mistakes. If the mistakes they want to make are particularly damaging, you may want to fight even harder, but remember it is not working.

Pick your stands. Odds are good that you are now feeling besieged and every move made by the bully is to be defended against. You are swinging wildly by now to protect yourself.

Stop doing that! Step back and ignore what is not important. The stuff that matters, you take a strong stand against. For example, if it is illegal or "Enron" bad, you state your position, and what you are prepared to do about it.

No righteousness. You simply state that you cannot support that choice and you may be forced to state your position to the board or whomever. You do not want to do this, but if they pursue this course, you will....

No more argument. It defuses the issue. Only response. Action. Not fear based, but strong.

It is almost guaranteed if you do this and get out of the battle, our friend the bully is likely to overplay his hand in his attempts to re-engage you. This war was about his incompetence. Without you to push against, he may have to face the music of his bad decisions. Rather than do that, it is more likely
that our bully may take on the boss. That is often what these wars are really about anyway!

Things to Remember:

1. STOP wallowing in the unfairness of everything. It is useless and self indulgent. Do you want to be a leader or remain a wimp?
2. Define your issues clearly. Refuse to engage in discussion over *anything* but your issues.
3. The battle is really between your enemy and your boss. It has been. Your bully is using you to gain advantage over your boss.
4. If you step out of the Game, your boss may have to decide if he or she is ready to play the Game.
5. Be prepared to act on your beliefs. This does not mean asking someone else to do something. It means taking action where the consequences are yours and you have stated that you are willing to accept them.
6. Get some dignity! Street fighting is not dignified.

Twelve

Techniques That Work

This chapter will present some basic techniques that work in a number of familiar Power Games to change the outcome to one that is healthier and more productive than what may be occurring now. There are some general rules which we have been emphasizing throughout this text, and then there are some specific techniques which work well with specific Power Games.

In terms of general rules that are important for any Power Game, first, learn to come from a sense of strength rather than weakness. The tone with which you deliver your response may be even more important than the words.

Second, deliver your response with class. Anything that approaches "common" is a bad idea. That means, no lectures, no shouting, no cursing, and no tears (would a person with high self-esteem cry when asking someone to stop pestering him or her?)

Third, in handling bullies, the most effective state of mind is detachment. Before you respond, be sure that you are not responding from emotion. Anger or fear will probably diminish the power of your response.

Remember, the Game is about dominance. A begging, pleading, cajoling attitude is about submission. You decide. Come from strength. Whether you believe you have potency or not, act as if you believe you have it.

Specific Approaches

The following list is meant to help you have an alternative in common situations. It is important to be conscious of the underlying reasons for these suggestions. Always come from Personal Power. These techniques are designed to help you to set boundaries, listen better, determine an outcome that is both gentle and definite, enhance the organizational well being while you handle a problem, and overall, leave you better off than you were when you were either not addressing the problem or addressing it badly.

For the Marshmallow:

> (*You*) If you know you are a marshmallow and tend to burst into tears, stutter, bluster or other ill-advised behavior under stress, it is very helpful to think of someone you know who is effective in similar situations. Simply pretend to be that person and see if it does not help you to remain more objective. For example, if you know someone who is emotionally very cool and detached in tough situations, you may want to emulate them. If there is someone you admire who manages to stay very logical and focused when someone is attacking, perhaps you will want to imagine that you are that person during a challenging moment.

For Arrogance:

There are a number of highly successful techniques for handling arrogant behavior. All of these techniques rely on *directness* as the essence for their effectiveness.

The Avoider: this is the person who doesn't want to meet with you for whatever reason. Rather than tell you, he or she allows you to get on the schedule and them simply cancels your appointments at the last minute.

Response: What you want is clarity. They are sending mixed messages. As always, being direct is the most useful technique. You might ask him or her if there is a reason that your appointments have been cancelled after they are scheduled. You might also ask him or her if you should take it personally. If you do not attack but are genuinely curious, there is no reason for him or her to respond badly. The person may either tell you the truth or may make something up to save face. Either way, this person now knows that you are interpreting the cancellations as directed at you.

Mr. or Ms. Superior: this person seems to insult you effortlessly by indicating in numerous ways that your job is less important than his or hers and that therefore, he or she should get preferential treatment.

Response: Again, the essence of the response is direct. In the moment, if you can do it without anger, stop the person and tell him or her how you have reacted to the tone or the comment which has offended you. You might also add that you want to think that this person did not mean to create that reaction in you, but that in fact, it has occurred and it is making you less receptive to whatever follows.

The Demander: this person demands that you do things for him or her, usually inappropriately and with no politeness.

Response: Same rule; be direct. It is always appropriate to say to a person that you would like to help, but you are resistant to the tone being used in general. If this person is repetitively obnoxious and has not responded to directness, you might simply try to say, nicely, "no thank you." This will often throw the person off balance because it is unexpected. To do so may up the odds of him or her hearing you when you are trying to communicate that you want to be treated with respect. This is because if you say that you want to be treated with respect, but you continue to do as this person demands even when you are uncomfortable, what they "hear" is that you will do it. Your displeasure is of no consequence to them.

If the person is your boss, you may want to try something a little different. You should decide how important it is to you that the person change behavior. If it is very important, you may want to set an appointment to talk. Give the person the benefit of the doubt. You may be supersensitive. Start the conversation by suggesting that you are very sensitive and you know that he or she probably is not aware that you are having a response to some of your interactions with each other.

You are hoping that he or she will simply slow down and ask slightly differently with an attention to the fact that you are there to do what is asked but that at times, you find yourself resisting because it feels unappreciated.

Remember, it is you who has the problem with this person's style. If you are not willing to take the risk to talk it through in a positive and problem solving way, stop your own negative reactions and do the work with a smile.

The Non-Responder: this person leads you to think that you have business together or a reason to communicate and then does not return your calls. This is often *not* just carelessness, but an attempt to assert dominance.

Response: You might try a note or a phone message that says, "Come out, come out wherever you are." This often gets a response. If you truly feel that it is part of a Power Game, you might simply be direct, "Perhaps you have changed your mind about working together." This causes the person to be clear with you in order that you are then able to move on if the circumstance has changed.

Mr. Nasty (or Ms): this is a person who truly does not play by the rules. He or she has no restraint when it comes to calling you or your ideas stupid, telling you that you add no value, or in general, simply being obnoxious.

Response: Direct, direct, direct. It is important that this type of behavior be stopped. It frequently escalates if your response is not definitive. You may find that you are often so completely surprised or frozen by the intensity of the attack that you do nothing or you react in kind. Also, respond to the attack not the issue. Too many good people find the dialogue deteriorates when they try to respond to the content of the attack.

For example, if a person attacks your idea as being stupid, it is seductive to attempt to defend the idea. There is no point in doing so because this person is not open to you or your idea in the first place and the others in the room are so uncomfortable with the tone of the conversation that they are also somewhat immune to your logic.

If someone calls your idea stupid, two things are happening. They are attacking you, not your idea. (There are lots of healthy ways to disagree about content.) Also, they are often attempting to divert attention from something they do not want to be accountable for and attacking you is a good way to keep everyone busy.

If instead of a useless defense of the idea, you respond by suggesting that you would like him or her to restate their objection to your concept more respectfully. You might also suggest very politely that it will be easier for you to remain objective to the comments if the comments are more clear and concise about what it is that is bothering him or her. If you are able to do so without condescension (respectfully), you may find that the whole tone changes and this person is now set up to do the right thing. The rest of the room is likely to be grateful for your Leadership as well.

Sneakiness: We have all dealt with the Snake. This person tells stories, changes stories, or makes up stories to suit him or herself. It is a Power Game with you if he or she is affecting you and your reputation, your Positional Power, or your comfort level with his or her tactics.

Response: Once again, directness is the best way to handle the snake. Ideally, if you know whom they have told their stories to, you mention it with that person in the room. You say, "I understand that you said .... Please correct me if I am wrong."

Because you chose to do it in the presence of the other person, they cannot deny it. They may be less likely to lie about you in the future.

Naturally the most difficult aspect of this is that the person who told you may not want it known that they talked to you about this. You may have to enlist their help with the understanding that the Snake will probably do this again and to others if he or she is not confronted. You may have to sell your friend on the value to the organization in doing so.

Annoyance: Some people act annoyed by you and your comments as a form of Power Game. If you ask them to do something, question their decision, or simply arrive in their presence, they act as though you have done something to annoy them. You know the behaviors. You just don't know why.

Response: You say, "I'm puzzled because you act annoyed that ...." This response usually causes them to explain themselves (which you need to hear) or to back off. This is a good technique to use with people in service industries who have forgotten that they are in business because of their customers.

Embarrass: There are those who take glee in embarrassing people as a way of dominating. They find your sensitivities and exploit them.

Response: There are so many forms of this kind of Power Game. The important thing to remember is that the other person has no sense of what is appropriate. His or her behaviors are telling you that *you* have not established appropriate boundaries. By attempting to humiliate or embarrass you, this person has told you that the "niceness" rule you would like to believe in is not being respected in this situation.

You would like the behavior to stop. Remember, this person wins if you feel embarrassed or humiliated by the comments or behavior. Instead of allowing this person to affect your own feelings of self, try to remember that he or she is the one that is acting inappropriately. Sometimes people embarrass or humiliate others because they feel awkward and use it as a way to mask their own feelings of discomfort.

If the embarrassment is in the form of pointing out your mistakes, you could again try directness. "You are right. I learned a lot".

It leaves them nowhere to go other than to truly act the buffoon. To hammer on someone who has admitted to making a mistake looks petty. If you argue or attempt to justify your behavior, you look defensive. Other than for the purpose of protecting your own ego, arguing serves no purpose.

If you find that you do not know what to say, perhaps because you are dumfounded by the behavior which attempts to humiliate or embarrass you, simply do nothing. It is a very safe response to simply look at the person and not respond. Silence is a very powerful tool. It allows the other person to think about what he or she has initiated. Some of the energy of whatever anger caused the initial action is dissipated. You have removed yourself as the target and the individual is left with his or her own confusion about what might have been the cause for the behavior.

Summary

There are so many forms of Power Games that we could do whole book on technique and it would not be enough. There are some basic fundamentals which can usually be applied successfully in most situations.

Things to Remember:

1. **Understanding your own weaknesses by examining the questions regarding Personal and Positional Power (these questions are identified in detail in chapters nine and ten), is key.**
2. **Directness regarding what you are feeling and why is a very effective tool for intervention in a Power Game.**

3. Humor is often a healthy technique for most situations, particularly when it is combined with directness.
4. When sucked into an unpleasant Power Game, detachment is often difficult but important to your ability to be effective. When you respond in anger or frustration, it usually escalates an already unpleasant situation. If detachment eludes you, take a breather before you respond.
5. Remember the law of cause and effect. If it works, do more of it. If it doesn't work, don't do more of it. Try something else.

Summary

Summary of Entire Text

This is just a beginning. Power Games are complicated, analysis is difficult, and winning is a sport requiring nothing less than mastery. There are however, just a couple of things to keep in mind if you choose to take the "road less traveled".

First, it isn't mastery unless it is done with an appearance of being effortless. Make the right things easy and the wrong things difficult. Your opponent should see the path of least resistance as the one that is also the most "Game friendly" path.

Remember the Rules. You want the outcome to be good for organization, good for participants, etc.. In other words, you set the Game up, and you set *you* up, in a way that doing the Right thing is the easiest and most rewarding path. Can you do that? Do you understand the Game well enough to do that?

If it was easy, everyone would be doing it. If you think of yourself as out of the ordinary, prove it by taking on the challenge of the Power Game. It is a long and endless study of all things human. The reward is a form of Personal Power that is recognizable as a Force by anyone who encounters you.

Review of Concepts in this Text

❏   Power Games are about Pecking Order!
❏   People have two kinds of Power: Personal Power and Positional Power.
❏   Everyone is a Force. The influence of your force is determined by the balance between your Personal and Positional Power.

- Increasing Positional Power does **nothing** to enhance the *quality* of your choices or outcomes.
- Increasing Personal Power has a lot to do with improving the **quality** of your choices and outcomes.
- Increasing Positional Power affects the **thrust** or force behind your choices and outcomes.
- Those who have Positional Power have a **responsibility** to be accountable for their Personal Power. Otherwise they are abusive.
- Representing people's Power Vectors on a two dimensional graph gives you a visual perspective of the outcome of the interactions between them.
- The visual represented by combining people's Power Vectors offers compelling evidence of the impact on the organization. The following diagrams represent the outcome of interactions between individuals.

What Happens When?

The following is a visual summary of what happens to the environment when various personalities interact.

Bully and a Bully Interact

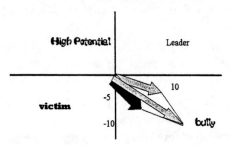

When bullies interact with each other in a culture they affect the entire culture. People are inspired to hone their bullying skills in order to survive and the culture becomes unsafe for any but the most determined of the nasty individuals who thrive in such a culture.

Leader Interacts with Leader

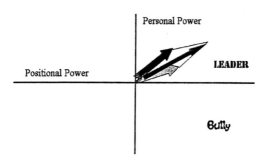

When leader interacts with leader the entire culture benefits. (Leaders are those who possess both Positional Power and Personal Power including wisdom, judgement, and superb communication skills.) Others are encouraged to follow suit. They are part of a team which is respectful, listens well, and exercises good judgement in the timing and execution of plans.

Bully and a Victim Interact

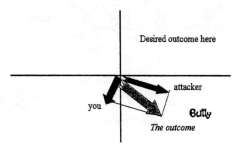

This graph in itself should be an incentive for those who turn into victims to understand that they have a responsibility to learn how to take on the bullies and stop being victims . When a bully is allowed to attack and defeat a victim, others are affected. The victim is abused but others become fearful that the bully will soon turn his attention to those who are left. The bully is often left unopposed and as the environment closes down, people stop communicating, and the quality of the entire business or organization is diminished due to the pall caused by the fear of annoying the bully who will probably have identified his or her own agenda.

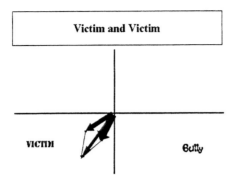

In an environment where victims are feeding off of each other the energy is low. Others are at fault for everything that goes wrong. It is a complete energy drain to people surrounding the victims as they spread their negative energy and sense of helplessness around. Most of us who have had the experience of working with or living with victims find the feeling to be oppressive at the very least.

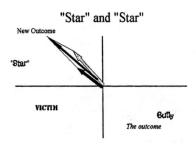

"Star" and "Star"

When High Potentials interact they create an expanded potential for the whole. Anyone who has ever worked on a team that was carefully created by finding people of highest potential may attest to the enhanced possibilities and energy involved when these folks get together. If you think of "Stars" as your High Potential players, you can see that their interaction creates an increased potential for the whole.

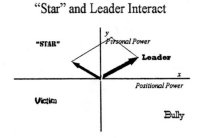

"Star" and Leader Interact

When a High Potential "Star" is fortunate enough to interact with a Leader, the organization, once again, benefits from the outcome. Often the "Star" is mentored and is given leadership responsibility early. The culture thrives on developing high quality individuals who have exhibited judgement and wisdom (remember their y value is high even if they do not yet have any rank.) Keep in mind, the actual magnitude of these arrows could be different (blue could be smaller than green) and the result could fall into High Potential. What this would mean is that if this Leader had less rank and was less able to bring the "Star" along as quickly, we would have a cultural effect of continuing to enhance the Potential of the organization. This is still a very positive outcome.

Victim and "Star" Interact

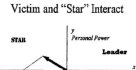

When a Victim interacts with a "Star" personality it may be a deflating experience. This often happens when an outsider, full of enthusiasm for change is brought into an organization where the players have learned to be victims. Over time, they sap the energy of the "Star" and the culture becomes more disheartened as a result. It is possible, if "Star" is more powerful in his or her magnitude than the Victim

107

(bigger green arrow), he or she may drag the result into the "Star"quadrant and the whole organization benefits.

Victim and Leader Interact

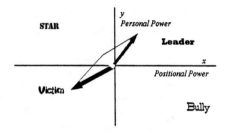

A Leader interacting with a Victim has the potential of creating more potential for the organization by influencing the result to the "Star"Quadrant. If however, the Victim is stronger than the Leader, the result could flip over to the Bully quadrant. The Victim, in his or her need to remain unaccountable, may create an outcome of non-accountability and excuses for poor performance. In this environment, Bullies tend to thrive.

In final summary, the adjustment of both magnitude and direction of any of the arrows in the above examples may shift the result for the culture of the organization dramatically. The changes in magnitude and direction of your Force in any Power Game depend on YOU!

There are things in *any* Power Game which you can do to swing the balance of Power to one that is more healthy and more productive.

APPENDIX

DETERMINING THE (*x,y*) VALUES FOR THE VECTORS

For *each* interaction between individuals or groups, you can ask a series of questions and you can determine an x value for each entity's Positional Power endpoint, and you can ask another set of questions to determine the y value for each entity's Personal Power endpoint.

The values of x range from -10 to +10 and the values of y from -10 to +10.

Questions to determine x

To what extent is this person's (Name:_____)Positional Power able to affect the outcome of this interaction? This will largely be determined by the following questions. Work through all the questions for each individual involved in the Power Game.

I.   Ability to manage perceptions.

14.   Relative to the other person or group involved in this Power Game, how does this person's Rank measure up?

- higher   10
- equal   5
- less than   - 5
- much less than   -10

2.   In this situation, the other individual's respect for this person's rank or Position is:

- high   10
- somewhat   5
- not much   - 5
- negative   -10

3.   In this specific situation, the *circumstance* enhances this person's Positional Power

- a great deal   10
- somewhat   5
- not much   - 5
- works to a disadvantage   -10

(An Example where circumstance might affect the Positional Power would be an intense labor negotiation where a walk out would be a disaster.)

4.   This person *believes* that his or her Position entitles him or her to win this Power Game:

- Absolutely   10
- To some degree   5
- May be something of a disadvantage - 5
- Clearly works against he or she   -10

II.   Ability to manage knowledge

    5.   In this situation, this person is considered an expert on the subject matter at hand.

        • To a great degree   10
        • To some degree   5
        • Has no advantage due to knowledge - 5
        • Lack of knowledge in this situation
          works against this person   -10

    6.   In this situation, while the person has expertise, his or her ability to influence this situation due to that expertise is:

        • very high   10
        • limited (influence)   5
        • may be somewhat of a disadvantage - 5
        • works against this person   -10

(example where expertise may not help would be one where this person is considered a "know it all" and people tune him or her out as a result of ineffective personal style)

III.   Ability to manage connections

    7.   This person has connections which have:

        • a great influence on this situation   10
        • some influence on this situation   5
        • may somewhat weaken this situation   - 5
        • a negative influence on this situation -10

8.   This person's ability to utilize his or her connections in this situation is:

●	very high	10
●	somewhat	5
●	of no help	- 5
●	complicates or worsens situation	-10

The x value is found by adding the 8 answers above and dividing by 8.

The mathematical result is the value for the horizontal component of this person's Power Vector in this situation.

Total Value for x is:_____

Questions to determine y

LXXVII.   Managing Fear

1.   To what extent is this person able to remain unafraid and relaxed in this situation?

●	completely relaxed and fearless	10
●	generally relaxed and unafraid	5
●	somewhat disturbed	- 5
●	tense and fearful	-10

2. To what extent do you believe this person is capable of hearing negative feedback regarding his or her behaviors or choices in this situation?

    - fully open   10
    - somewhat willing to listen   5
    - closed to comment   - 5
    - very negative reaction to feedback   -10

3. To what degree does this person exhibit self-esteem in this situation. by his or her ability to establish appropriate boundaries?

    - fully self-confident   10
    - generally confident in self   5
    - very little confidence in self   5
    - let's others walk all over boundaries -10

4. To what degree is this person able to know when it is time to act and when it is time to wait?

    - extremely decisive and effective in addressing needs in a timely manner.   10
    - somewhat capable in addressing needs and responding appropriately   5
    - generally too quick or too slow to respond   -5
    - is likely to act counter to needs   -10

II. Managing Confusion

5. To what degree is this person capable of being totally honest with self and others in this situation?

- extremely straightforward   10
- generally honest and direct   5
- generally evasive or passive   -5
- likely to lie to protect self   -10

6. How likely is this person to act with integrity in this situation?

- extremely   10
- somewhat   5
- not very likely   -5
- unlikely   -10

7. How capable is this person of asking questions and listening (objectively) to the other person this situation?

- extremely   10
- somewhat   5
- not very open   -5
- adverse to hearing comments   -10

8. To what degree is this person capable of analyzing the cause and effect relationships between his or her actions and the results?

- extremely conscious of relationship 10
- somewhat capable of recognition 5
- not very likely to make the connection -5
- mis-assesses cause and effect frequently -10

III. Managing Arrogance

9. To what degree is this person balanced enough to keep this situation in perspective?

- extremely clear 10
- generally balanced 5
- not comfortable -5
- easily destabilized -10

10. How capable is this person of keeping a longer term agenda in view while acting out of short-term need?

- maintains long term view throughout 10
- generally able to keep perspective 5
- not very likely to see beyond the moment -5
- totally engaged in task at hand -10

11. To what degree is this person able to think in terms of the other person's needs while dealing with his or her own?

- extremely aware 10
- generally conscious 5
- not very concerned -5
- totally oblivious -10

12. How conscious is this person regarding the needs of the entire organization when choosing how to respond to situations?

- extremely aware   10
- generally conscious   5
- not very concerned   - 5
- totally oblivious beyond personal needs -10

The value of the y component is found by adding the answers to the 12 questions and dividing by 12.

The mathematical result is the value of the vertical component of the person's Power Vector.

The Total Y Value is: _____

Finding the Power Vectors

To find each person's power vector, draw the line from the point $(0,0)$ to the (x,y) values you determined by asking the above questions.

After you have drawn each person's Power Vector, you can find the outcome by adding the two x values to determine x of the new vector, and adding the two y values to determine y of the new vector. OR, you simply complete the parallelogram.

A Simple (x,y) Graph

y=Personal Power

(0, 0)

x=Positional Power

Other Works by Toni Lynn Chinoy

What To Do When It Rains, a handbook for leaders in crisis. This book is the first volume in this series. As a stand-alone it is a very powerful book on the fundamentals of leadership. With a foreword by Ann McLaughlin, chairman of the Aspen Institute, it is a must read for all students of leadership. This book sits by the bedside of many well-known leaders, due to its practical insight into issues of relationships and decision-making for individuals and groups seeking to get above the chaos.

What To Do When It Rains, a handbook for organizations in crisis. This is the sequel to Part I and continues the story of the Sorot Corporation. The focus in this text is on the corporation itself and helps leaders to identify and solve problems affecting the long term health of the organization.

Perfect Speed. Perfect Speed is a short book that helps the reader explore his or her own potential and the belief systems standing in the way of achieving the most exciting and fulfilling of possibilities.

The War Between the Whirligigs and the Tanks. This short book helps the reader understand and more effectively handle clashes between two distinct personality types. How does a Whirligig (the most free and risk taking of individuals) maintain respect and engage effectively with the Tank (the type of individual who is dedicated to planning and thinking through actions to arrive at the most safe and powerful of outcomes)? This text will help your work relationships as well as your personal relationships.

On Women, Leadership and Evolution This short text is written specifically for women who are doing the work on self necessary for fulfilled and peaceful lives. The book addresses the issues of professional and personal lives from the perspective of wanting and having it all.

In Search of a Yatz, a love story. This is a novel written for anyone who has lost at love. This charming story offers a deeper meaning for those too important relationships that sometimes distract us from our purpose in life. A combination between a myth and reality, this story is a must read for anyone determined to figure out the ups and downs of personal relationships.

Call us toll free at our Harlan-Evans, Inc and Catapult Press headquarters at 866-949-2734 or visit us at our web site www.harlanevans.com .

For timely, fun coaching on Leadership issues, please visit our coaching web site at www.corporatewizards.com Check out how you can become a member and have access through e-mail to an executive coach.

Any one who spends a portion of his or her life traveling for business might enjoy *Poems of the Corporate Wars,* by Marc Paul Chinoy, also published by Catapult Press.

Catapult Press, Inc
36105 Charles Town Pike
Purcellville, VA   20132

Phone: 540-668-7158